THE LITTLE BOOK OF

PROSECCO

TIPS

Andrew Langley

THE LITTLE BOOK OF

PROSECCO

TIPS

BLOOMSBURY ABSOLUTE

LONDON · OXFORD · NEW YORK · NEW DELHI · SYDNEY

'He wanted death to take him just at the moment he laid his last lira down on a bar and said, "Prosecco for everyone".'

Donna Leon,
Friends in High Places

1. **Prosecco = fun.** It's a cheerful sparkling wine that's meant to be enjoyed. The perfect aperitif, it perks up the taste buds and stimulates the appetite without overloading the palate. All the same, it should be treated with respect. At its best it is a wonderful wine, so **buy the best you can afford**.

"Prosecco = fun. Buy the best you can afford."

2. **How can you tell one Prosecco from another?** Look at the label. The cheapest and lowest quality stuff bears the initials IGT. If it says DOC, it was produced in Prosecco's designated geographical area in northeast Italy. If it's DOCG, it is from one specific part of that area, and is of higher quality still – and pricier.

"How can you tell one Prosecco from another?"

3. You'll know **you've hit the jackpot if you see the words** *Superiore di Cartizze* **on a Prosecco label!** This is the greatest expression of these wines, produced in the hills round the Cartizze Valley in the centre of the Prosecco region. Drink it whenever you find it.

"You've hit the jackpot if you see the words *Superiore di Cartizze* on a Prosecco label!"

4. **Chill your Prosecco well before drinking it.** A cold sparkling wine forms smaller bubbles which last longer once it is opened and poured. Put the bottle in the fridge for three hours at a temperature of 6–9°C.

Chill your Prosecco well before drinking it.

5. Be tender with your bottles of Prosecco; remember that the liquid inside is under surprisingly high pressure. **Handle bottles of Prosecco gently and keep them out of the freezer** – even if you're in a hurry. The shock of the extreme cold can spoil both the taste and the fizz.

"Handle bottles of Prosecco gently and keep them out of the freezer."

6. **Only chill Prosecco if you're going to drink it fairly soon.** Otherwise, remove all bottles from the fridge. Long term, the very cold air affects the flavour and dries out the corks, causing them to shrink. And vibrations from the motor and the slamming door could create further damage.

"Only chill Prosecco if you're going to drink it fairly soon."

7.

Why the name? **It originally took its title from the village of Prosecco, near where it was first made**. The main grape variety became known as 'Prosecco' too. However, the Italian government recently ruled that the 'Prosecco' should refer only to the specific region in which it is made. The grape was renamed Glera. Confused?

"It originally took its title from the village of Prosecco, near where it was first made."

8. Sparkling wine is almost always served in narrow flute glasses. But, **if you are drinking a high-end Prosecco, try a slightly wider, more bowl-shaped glass**. This allows the wine to breathe better than a flute, and the floral aromas to gather and concentrate. Tulip-shaped glasses are best of all.

"If you are drinking a high-end Prosecco, try a slightly wider more bowl-shaped glass."

9. Beware soap! **Make sure your glasses are washed thoroughly after use and then rinsed well.** Any lingering traces of detergent will wreak havoc with Prosecco bubbles, leaving you with a flat flabby wine. Lipstick, olive oil and other fatty substances pose a similar threat.

Make sure your glasses are washed thoroughly after use and then rinsed well.

10.

A bottle of bubbly can be an offensive weapon – especially when being opened. So point it at the ceiling, rather than other people. **Remove the foil and untwist the wire muzzle.** Put a tea towel over the cork. Grip the cork through the towel and **gently twist the bottle (not the cork)**. It should come out with a quiet pop and hiss.

"Remove the foil and untwist the wire muzzle. Gently twist the bottle (not the cork)."

11. **Sometimes** – even in strong hands – **the cork refuses to move. Encourage it by pushing the wide lip upwards** with your thumbs, taking care not to snap the top off. If all else fails, a corkscrew or even a pair of pliers will do the trick. But remember: once loosened, a stuck stopper can fly out like a bullet.

"Sometimes the cork refuses to move. Encourage it by pushing the wide lip upwards."

12.

Pouring sparkling wine is an art – after all, millions of litres of Prosecco are wasted every year from overfrothing glasses. So be patient. Start with a small amount in a glass. When the bubbles subside, **tilt the glass and fill it by sliding the wine down the side** without any splashing.

"Pouring sparkling wine is an art. Tilt the glass and fill it by sliding the wine down the side.

13.

When drinking, **hold your glass by the stem or, better still, by the base**. This helps the wine to stay chilled. Wrap your fingers round the bowl, and your body heat will warm the wine and make it lose fizz more quickly.

"Hold your glass by the stem or, better still, by the base."

14.

Believe it or not, **you may** occasionally **be left with a half-drunk bottle** of Prosecco. Pushing in an old cork is not a reliable preservation method. Instead, **re-seal with a hinged bubble stopper or with cling film secured by a rubber band** and keep in the fridge. It could stay fizzy for up to a week.

"You may be left with a half-drunk bottle. Re-seal with a hinged bubble stopper or with cling film secured by a rubber band."

15.

Prosecco makes the ideal base for countless cocktails. These often involve fruit, syrup or some other sweetener. So it's worth using a dry version (look for the words 'Brut' or even 'Extra Brut' on the label) to give a bit of contrast and bite to the mixture.

"Prosecco makes the ideal base for countless cocktails."

16.

Other sparklers #1: Cava. There are lots of other competitively priced sparkling wines on the market besides Prosecco. The best-known is Cava, which comes mostly from southern Spain. More robust than Prosecco, it can be used as a substitute in many cocktails.

"Other sparklers #1: Cava."

17. **The grandaddy of Prosecco cocktails is the Spritz Veneziano**, or spritz for short. Put a measure of a bitter Italian drink such as Campari, Aperol or Cynar in a big wine glass. Add Prosecco and top up with sparkling mineral water and a slice of orange.

"The grandaddy of Prosecco cocktails is the Spritz Veneziano.

18.

Invented in a Venetian bar in the 1930s, **the classic Bellini cocktail is named after the painter Giovanni Bellini**. Skin and purée some ripe white peaches and chill well. Combine 1 part peach purée to 2 parts Prosecco in an old-fashioned champagne glass.

"The classic Bellini cocktail is named after the painter Giovanni Bellini."

19.

Plenty **more celebrated Italians have now joined the great Prosecco cocktail party**, based on different fruits. There's the Rossini, which uses strawberry purée instead of peach, and the Puccini (mandarin juice), while the splendid Tintoretto calls for pomegranate juice.

" More celebrated Italians have now joined the great Prosecco cocktail party. "

20. **For a more antique Italian cocktail, try a Sgroppino**, which means 'a loosening up' or 'untying' – what your stomach needs after a heavy second course. Whisk two good scoops of lemon sorbet (softened a bit) with a slug of vodka. Add Prosecco, stirring very gently to preserve the fizz, until just pourable.

"For a more antique Italian cocktail, try a Sgroppino."

21.

The French 77 is a jollier version of the famous French 75 champagne cocktail – and not French at all! Swirl 1 tablespoon of elderflower liqueur and the juice of half a lemon in a glass. Top up with well-chilled Prosecco and serve with a twist of lemon zest.

"The French 77 is a jollier version of the famous French 75 champagne cocktail."

22.

Great cocktails can be created by mistake. A Milan barman was asked for a Negroni cocktail, and accidentally added sparkling wine instead of gin. The result – the Sbagliato ('messed up') – was an instant classic. Simply mix equal parts of Campari, Red Vermouth and Prosecco over ice, and add a slice of orange.

"Great cocktails can be created by mistake."

23.

Other sparklers #2: cremant.
This French wine is produced by the same method as Champagne, but outside the Champagne region in places such as the Loire, Burgundy and Alsace. The name means 'creamy', which conveys its classy smoothness and quality.

"Other sparklers #2: cremant."

24.

Prosecco and sloe gin? They **are unlikely but sensational partners.** Shake up a slug of sloe gin, the juice of half a lemon plus 1 egg white in a cocktail shaker. Add crushed ice and shake a bit more. Strain into glasses and top up with Prosecco. The egg white gives a lovely frothiness.

"Prosecco and sloe gin are unlikely but sensational partners.

25. Here are **two legendary Italian drinks in one glass**. Wipe lemon juice and sugar round a glass's rim. Put in 1 tablespoon of Limoncello and 2 teaspoons of lemon juice, and pop in a roll of lemon zest. Fill up with Prosecco (slowly, so as not to froth up).

"Two legendary Italian drinks in one glass...

26. On a hot day, **treat yourself to a summer fruit cocktail**. Crush blueberries, strawberries, blackberries and mint leaves in a jug. Add a dollop of Cassis and stir it all together. Dole out into glasses and put a slug of vodka and some ice in each. Top up with Prosecco.

"Treat yourself to a summer fruit cocktail."

27. **Other sparklers #3: reds.**
Exciting possibilities here.
Frothing, off-dry Lambrusco
from Italy has shaken off its naff
past and is now worth exploring.
Australian sparkling Shiraz can
be nicely fruity and peppery.
For a rarer treat, look out for
'Pearl of Azerbaijan' from
Eastern Europe.

“Other sparklers #3: reds.”

28. Simplest Prosecco cocktail ever? **A sparkling Mimosa needs only two ingredients – orange juice and Prosecco**. But the juice must be freshly squeezed AND well chilled in the fridge. Pour the wine in the glass first, then add an equal measure of orange juice (this prevents too much froth).

"A sparkling Mimosa needs only two ingredients – orange juice and Prosecco."

29.

Prosecco perks you up – even when it's icy outside. **For a fizzy winter warmer, shake up a slug of whisky, a dash of Chartreuse,** the **juice of half a lemon, and** 1 teaspoon of **honey** in a cocktail shaker. **Strain** into a glass **and top up with Prosecco.**

"For a fizzy winter warmer, shake up a slug of whisky, a dash of Chartreuse, juice of half a lemon and honey. Strain and top up with Prosecco."

30.

Prosecco – like most wines – **is a fine ingredient in cooking. There are just two rules to remember.** One: if you would happily drink Prosecco with a dish, then you can use Prosecco in cooking that dish. And two: a dish can easily be spoiled by using low-grade wine in the cooking. Use the best you can.

"Prosecco is a fine ingredient in cooking. There are just two rules to remember..."

31.

Prosecco goes beautifully with chicken. In a large casserole, brown floured chicken pieces and pancetta in olive oil. Remove to a plate. Now sauté halved shallots, 1 chopped red chilli and chopped rosemary. Return the chicken, add a bottle of Prosecco and cook gently for 30 minutes. Season to taste.

"**Prosecco goes beautifully with chicken.**"

32.

Other sparklers #4: American bubbly. The US is mainly free from restrictive laws about how sparkling wine can be made. The result is a huge and very variable choice, including many great rosé wines. Look out for sparklers from California, New York State and New Mexico.

"Other sparklers #4:
American bubbly."

33.

Prosecco has a sweetness which perfectly complements seafood. For oysters, there's mignonette sauce. Mix equal proportions of white wine vinegar and chopped shallots in a glass bowl. After 10 minutes, stir in another equal part of Prosecco. Pour sparingly on shucked oysters.

"Prosecco has a sweetness which perfectly complements seafood."

34.

Prosecco fondue sounds crazy but tastes terrific. Gently warm 225ml of Brut Prosecco in a pan with 1 tablespoon of cornflour. Then stir in 220g of Brie or a similar soft cheese. Add pinches of nutmeg and cinnamon, plus 1 teaspoon of lemon juice, and finally a slug of schnapps. Get dipping.

"Prosecco fondue sounds crazy but tastes terrific."

35. **Prosecco and porcini gravy goes beautifully with roast chicken.** Soak a pack of dried porcini in warm water for 2 hours. Soften chopped onion and garlic in butter, then add 4 parts chicken stock to 1 part Prosecco. Pop in fresh thyme, plus the porcini (sliced) and their juices. Simmer for 20 minutes.

"Prosecco and porcini gravy goes beautifully with roast chicken."

36. **Cook mussels with a good Brut Prosecco** – the wine's flavour comes through. Sauté chopped garlic and spring onion in butter for 30 seconds, then pour in half a bottle of Prosecco. When it boils, add mussels which have been cleaned and well-prepared. They should be open and ready in another 3 minutes.

"Cook mussels with a good Brut Prosecco.

37.

Baked or roast fish demands something buttery and exotic. **Prosecco butter sauce is the answer.** Simmer 3 minced shallots hard in half a bottle of fizz for 15 minutes. Remove from the heat and whisk in 150g of butter, chunk by chunk. Add ground pepper. Perfect with salmon or cod fillet.

"Prosecco butter sauce is the answer."

38. It's a lot more than an aperitif! Prosecco can be drunk happily with all kinds of food. A good quality Brut has a citrus zing which enhances the taste of fish and other seafood (especially pasta and rice dishes). **The slight acidity of the Extra Dry perfectly suits soft cheeses and poultry.**

"The slight acidity of the Extra Dry perfectly suits soft cheeses and poultry."

39.

Other sparklers #5: English. A warmer climate means riper grapes, which is why English (and Welsh) wines are on the up and sparkling whites are leading the charge. Many of these are very high quality, deliciously dry and acidic. There are plenty of affordable examples if you hunt for them.

"Other sparklers #5: English."

40. **Zabaione is even more delicious made with bubbly.** Beat 5 egg yolks in a bowl over simmering water. Add cinnamon, then Prosecco, drop by drop and beating constantly (about 10 tablespoons). Once creamy, remove from the heat and keep beating. Spoon into glasses and add whipped cream.

"Zabaione is even more delicious made with bubbly."

41.

Here's a delectable and simple strawberry and Prosecco sorbet. Make a syrup by simmering 250g of sugar in 125ml of water. Hull 450g of strawberries and whizz briefly in a processor. Add in the cooled syrup plus 2 glasses of Prosecco and mix until smooth. Pour into a plastic tub and freeze.

"Here's a delectable and simple strawberry and Prosecco sorbet..."

42.

Bubbly jelly with real bubbles! Chill wine glasses in the freezer. Then heat 2 tablespoons of water with 50g of sugar. Stir in 1 tablespoon of gelatine powder and let cool. Add half a bottle of Prosecco, pour the mixture into the glasses and return to the freezer for 30 minutes. Dot with raspberries.

"Bubbly jelly with real bubbles!"

43.

Give angel cake a heavenly boost with rose and Prosecco syrup. Heat half a bottle of Prosecco with 300g of sugar and a vanilla pod. After a 5 minute simmer, stir in the juice of half a lemon and 3 teaspoons of rosewater. When it's cool, slice the cake horizontally and layer with the syrup and mascarpone.

"Give angel cake a heavenly boost with rose and Prosecco syrup.

44.

Prosecco jam – it's the new marmalade! Whizz up 10 peeled clementines and put in a preserving pan. Pour in 600g of sugar, the juice of a lemon and 3 glasses of Prosecco. Boil up and simmer until it reaches its setting point (about 45 minutes). Store in sterilised jars.

"Prosecco jam – it's the new marmalade!"

45. **Prosecco has even inspired an Italian version of the classic Black Velvet cocktail.** Its name? Italian Velvet, or 'Velluto Italiano'. Simply mix 2 parts Italian beer, such as Birra Moretti or Birra del Borgo, with 1 part Prosecco.

"Prosecco has even inspired an Italian version of the classic Black Velvet cocktail."

46. Turn leftover Prosecco and cheese scraps into something yummy. **Chop up the cheese and blend with the wine and a chunk of butter in a processor.** Adjust proportions until you have a smooth, spreadable consistency. Lastly **whizz in chopped parsley. Perfect for sandwiches.**

"Chop up the cheese and blend with the wine and a chunk of butter in a processor. Whizz in chopped parsley. Perfect for sandwiches."

47.

Drink it up! Prosecco, unlike vintage Champagne, does not age in the bottle. On the contrary, **all except the very highest quality Prosecco goes stale within three years** at the most. So you just have to **drink it as young as possible**. Go on, force yourself.

"All except the very highest quality Prosecco goes stale within three years. Drink it as young as possible."

48.

Keep bottles on their sides to prevent the corks from drying out and shrinking. Preferably, store your sparkling wines away from direct sunlight, somewhere that is cool and stays at a steady temperature. This prevents pressure and quality changes inside the bottle.

"Keep bottles on their sides to prevent the corks from drying out and shrinking."

49. **Need some chilled Prosecco in a hurry?** Instead of bunging a bottle in the freezer, get out an ordinary bucket. Half-fill it with ice, pour on a cup of salt and water to cover and stir it all up. Pop the Prosecco down into the icy slush and it'll be chilled in 15 minutes.

“**Need some chilled Prosecco in a hurry?**”

50.

Not all Prosecco is sparkling
(*spumante* in Italian). If you're in the
Prosecco region of Italy, look out for
the less usual *frizzante*, which is only
lightly fizzy (more a prickle than
a bubble). Then there is *tranquillo*
(still), which has no bubbles at all,
and is now growing in popularity.

"Not all Prosecco is sparkling."

Andrew Langley

Andrew Langley is **a knowledgeable food and drink writer.** Among his formative influences he lists a season picking grapes in Bordeaux, several years of raising sheep and chickens in Wiltshire and two decades drinking his grandmother's tea. He has written books on a number of Scottish and Irish whisky distilleries and is the editor of the highly regarded anthology of the writings of the legendary Victorian chef Alexis Soyer.

"A knowledgeable food and drink writer."

**Little Books of Tips from
Bloomsbury Absolute**

Aga	Gin
Allotment	Golf
Avocado	Herbs
Beer	Prosecco
Cake Decorating	Rum
Cheese	Spice
Cider	Tea
Coffee	Vodka
Fishing	Whisky
Gardening	Wine

If you enjoyed this book, try...

THE LITTLE BOOK OF

GIN

TIPS

"An adults-only take on a childhood treat, try this gin and tonic float..."

"Great gin pairings #2: fiery ginger beer."

BLOOMSBURY ABSOLUTE
Bloomsbury Publishing Plc
50 Bedford Square, London, WC1B 3DP, UK

BLOOMSBURY, BLOOMSBURY ABSOLUTE, the Diana logo and the Absolute Press
logo are trademarks of Bloomsbury Publishing Plc

First published in Great Britain 2019
Copyright © Andrew Langley, 2019
Cover image © Polly Webster, 2019

A catalogue record for this book is available from the British Library.
Library of Congress Cataloguing-in-Publication data has been applied for.

ISBN: 9781472973320
2 4 6 8 10 9 7 5 3 1

Printed and bound in China by Toppan Leefung Printing

Bloomsbury Publishing Plc makes every effort to ensure that the papers used in the
manufacture of our books are natural, recyclable products made from wood grown in
well-managed forests. Our manufacturing processes conform to the environmental
regulations of the country of origin.
    To find out more about our authors and books visit www.bloomsbury.com and sign
up for our newsletters.